GENERAL EDITOR DENNIS RAINEY

preparing for marriage

Leader's Guide

BY DAVID BOEHI, BRENT NELSON
JEFF SCHULTE & LLOYD SHADRACH

Gospel Light
The Bible. Pure and Simple.

Published by Gospel Light
Ventura, California, U.S.A.
www.gospellight.com
Printed in the U.S.A.

Library of Congress Cataloging-in-Publication Data
Preparing for marriage : leader's guide / David Boehi ... [et al.] ; Dennis Rainey, general editor.
p. cm.
Includes bibliographical references.
ISBN 978-0-8307-4641-5 (trade paper)
1. Marriage—Religious aspects—Christianity—Study and teaching. I. Boehi, David.
II. Rainey, Dennis, 1948-
BV835.P733 2010
248.4071—dc22
2010002993

Rights for publishing this book outside the U.S.A. or in non-English languages are
administered by Gospel Light Worldwide, an international not-for-profit ministry.
For additional information, please visit www.glww.org, email info@glww.org, or write to
Gospel Light Worldwide, 1957 Eastman Avenue, Ventura, CA 93003, U.S.A.

To order copies of this book and other Gospel Light products in bulk quantities,
please contact us at 1-800-446-7735.

Contents

About This Course

Preparing for Marriage was developed by a group of men working with FamilyLife, a subsidiary of Campus Crusade for Christ. FamilyLife's goal is to help you learn practical, biblical blueprints for building a godly home. FamilyLife outreaches include:

"FamilyLife Today": a 30-minute radio program featuring Dennis Rainey, FamilyLife executive director and the general editor of this study. The show airs five days a week on hundreds of stations across the country.

The Weekend to Remember marriage conferences: weekend getaways for couples that have changed the lives of hundreds of thousands of couples since 1976.

The HomeBuilders Couples Series: a group of small-group Bible studies to help married couples grow in their relationship.

For more information about FamilyLife, visit our website at FamilyLife.com, call 1-800-FL-TODAY, or write us at 5800 Ranch Drive, Little Rock, AR 72223.

A Message to Mentors from Dennis Rainey

Consider for a moment the training that most teenagers receive to qualify for a driver's license. At the age of 15 (in most states), they can receive a driver's permit if they pass a written test of their knowledge of the state's driving laws. During the next year, they drive under the supervision of a parent or adult. If they are wise, they complete a driver's education course. Through hours of practice, they slowly learn the hundreds of small skills that skillful driving requires: how to accelerate and brake under different conditions, what to observe while driving down a road, how to turn onto a street or into a parking space, and so much more.

Finally, they must prove their skill by passing a driver's test administered by a state-licensed examiner. Now they have a prized driver's license in their hands . . . only to learn that several years of safe driving will be required until they shed the costly mistrust harbored by at least one segment of society—the car insurance companies!

Now consider the requirements for obtaining another type of license. To be legally married, a couple must obtain a blood test and must state their vows of commitment before an ordained minister or a justice of the peace. That's it. If they are wise, they will receive some premarriage counseling, but in many churches that means little more than meeting with a pastor to go over the wedding procedures.

What's wrong with this picture?

Our society requires intensive training to receive a driver's license for one simple reason: We know that *bad things happen* when we allow someone to drive a car without first learning some critical skills.

Unfortunately, our society is only now waking up to the fact that *bad things happen* when we allow a couple to be married without learning some critical skills. I could spend pages analyzing all the reasons why America's divorce rate has been the highest of any country in the world for the last 30 years, but the reasons boil down to this: People don't know how to be married.

Children are growing up in a culture that emphasizes individuality over responsibility. Many are raised in fractured families. Because of this they don't learn the skills needed to relate to another person on a daily basis through good times and bad, in good health or poor, during times of plenty and times of need. They don't learn how to give or experience unconditional love in a marriage relationship, and our culture and our nation is suffering because of it.

That is why we have developed *Preparing for Marriage* and this accompanying leader's guide. We need to help families learn how to put God at the center of their lives and turn to His Word as their guide. The best time to do this is before couples get married—before they start to "drive on the streets."

There are few ministries in a church more strategic or effective than guiding couples through premarriage preparation. With the *Preparing for Marriage* workbook, you can help couples build their homes on the foundation of God's Word.

Notes on the Updated Edition

Since *Preparing for Marriage* was first published in 1997, we have been pleased to see hundreds of thousands of couples go through the workbook, usually with the help of a pastor, mentor or counselor. We often hear stories of how this resource is being used around the world. A friend says his two nieces went through the workbook at their church. A mentor couple writes to describe ministry they've helped build at their church, where dozens of couples complete the workbook each year and other singles are asking to go through the course even though they aren't in a serious relationship. Another man writes to say he has taken more than 40 couples through the workbook in Kenya. One of the couples told him they had "the best premarital counseling in Nairobi. We're determined that everyone we know goes through the same program."

In many ways the new, updated edition of the workbook and leader's guide are so similar to the original that you may not notice they have changed. The biggest changes were in format. We received a great deal of feedback that couples and mentors were often confused by all the different sections, chapters and projects in the original workbook. At times they didn't understand the order in which these elements should be completed.

Through some strategic reorganization, we have retained all the original material, but it is now much easier to follow. You simply take couples through the book in the order the material is presented in the workbook:

- ♥ Couples first complete two worksheets, "Understanding Your Personal History" and "Great Expectations."
- ♥ Couples then complete each of the eight chapters in numerical order.
- ♥ Two bonus projects—"Parental Wisdom Questionnaire" and "Couple Interview"—are offered in appendix A and appendix B. These are recommended but not required.

The Ultimate Marriage Preparation Guide

I'll never forget a woman who came to me one time for counseling after her divorce. Thinking back, she said, "As I was preparing for marriage it was as though I started out on this desert landscape. I picked up the binoculars and looked out on the horizon and I could see all of these corpses and all of the rotting flesh and the destruction of broken marriages that had not made it very far across the desert. And even though I could see that so many people hadn't made it very far, I didn't have anyone in my life to grab me by the shoulders and say,

'You need survival training before you start out.' So I started out on the journey with my husband, and after a few years had passed, I found myself in the same condition as those other people who had failed in their relationships."

There are two things I noticed about her comments. First, *she realized that premarriage training would have helped prepare her for the inevitable trials she would face in her marriage.* Many engaged couples today are apprehensive about this commitment they're about to make. Yes, they may act like they know it all, and they may be so consumed with planning a 30-minute ceremony and a two-hour reception that you'd think they wouldn't make the time for premarriage counseling. But they could—with a little encouragement. An increasing number come from broken families themselves, and they want to have successful marriages.

Preparing for Marriage provides the training they need. In fact, it includes the type of material Barbara and I wish we had known before our wedding. By completing *Preparing for Marriage,* couples will:

- ♥ Learn about how to make a good decision to marry—how to evaluate their relationship and how to discern God's will.
- ♥ Discover the joy of knowing each other and being known at levels they never imagined.
- ♥ Talk about things they never dreamed they would discuss but always knew they should.
- ♥ Anticipate issues ahead of time instead of being caught off guard after they are married.
- ♥ Know, apply and experience God's Word as it relates to engagement and marriage.
- ♥ Become confident, certain and secure in their decision to marry (or not to marry).
- ♥ Practice and apply foundational skills they need to build their marriage.
- ♥ Acquire some essential communication and conflict resolution skills.

♥ Understand the critical nature of core responsibilities in marriage.

♥ Learn about God's design for true sexual intimacy.

The Value of a Mentor

The second thing I noticed about the woman I counseled was that *she wished someone had been there to give her the type of help she needed.* It was as though she were saying that she needed someone in her life who understood what her needs were and could come alongside with love and compassion—not to preach, but to coach her and help her prepare for her journey. This person didn't have to be a pastor or counselor; it could have been an older married friend, or someone from her church—someone willing to take the time to prepare a young woman and a young man for a lifetime of marriage.

Whether you are a pastor, a counselor or a lay mentor couple, I am confident you will find this material easy to use as you work with premarried couples. It will guide you systematically through the key issues couples need to learn and discuss before marriage.

Plus, you will find your involvement personally enriching and rewarding as you sit down with a young couple and prepare them for marriage.

Don't assume you need seminary training to guide a couple through this material. All you need is to be available. Lay couples can provide a valuable help to their pastors by getting involved in premarried training. In some cases, these lay couples may even be able to teach these couples more than the pastors could, because they may have more time to devote to these couples.

Preparing to Lead

To guide a couple through *Preparing for Marriage,* you will need to read carefully through the workbook and through this

mentor's guide. The main chapters and the worksheets are designed so that you have several options for leading it:

- ♥ You can have a couple complete the main sessions on
  their own and then meet with you for discussion (this
  appears to be the most frequently used option).
- ♥ You can guide a couple personally through the main
  sessions and have them complete the Couple's Projects
  on their own.
- ♥ You can even guide a *small group* of couples through the
  main sessions and have them complete the Couple's
  Projects on their own.

However you use this material, we are confident that you will
find premarriage training a great adventure. You don't need years
of training. You don't need a special degree. All you need is the
willingness to be available—to teach, to train, to model, to encourage. You can do it, with Christ's help!

preparing for marriage
leader's guide

Chapter I

Overview of *Preparing for Marriage*

Goals

As we created *Preparing for Marriage*, our first goal was to *put together a quality, entertaining and thorough premarried curriculum that provides premarried couples the most important information and training they need before marriage.* Part of the material for this study was adapted from FamilyLife's Weekend to Remember™ marriage conferences. But we also developed additional material based on what we learned from interviews with premarried couples, pastors and premarital counselors.

We have found that many couples get married with only a scant understanding of how to build a relationship based on God's blueprint for the home. That's why we devote two chapters in the workbook to God's purposes and plan for marriage, and then another four chapters to topics important for couples starting marriage: communication, responsibilities of a husband and wife, finances and sexual intimacy.

Our second goal was to encourage couples to interact over what they're learning and apply the principles to their relationship. The narrative in each chapter is often broken by practical questions, and then each chapter ends with an interactive Couples Project. We also include two worksheets that help couples talk about the past and about their expectations for marriage. As you will see, this course requires a good deal of homework involving both personal study and couple interaction. This material raises important questions and helps couples address difficult issues. We've found that couples enjoy the time together and are grateful to discuss important topics they had not previously discussed together.

A third goal was to *challenge couples to seriously and honestly evaluate whether God really is calling them to marriage.* Let's be honest: It's very difficult for most couples to keep their heads clear during courtship and engagement. Many couples are so swept up in the emotions that they fail to take time to honestly evaluate their relationship and decide whether God is calling them together. Chapters 3 and 4 focus on these topics.

After completing the course, many couples will discover that God has used the material to reveal His direction or to confirm their decision. Some, however, will decide that they should postpone or cancel their wedding. Such decisions are difficult, but they protect these couples from a great deal of heartache down the road.

Our fourth and final goal was to *provide couples with the opportunity to learn and receive guidance from a pastor, counselor or mentoring couple.* Couples always begin marriage with a vow to make it work. But many unknowingly repeat many of the same errors their parents made, and they end up with a marriage far from what they had envisioned.

We are convinced that if churches want to help couples build strong marriages and families, they need to connect couples with godly older mentors who have already been down the same path. These mentors may be pastors or trained counselors, but they don't need to be. If you are walking with God, and if your marriage is on solid ground, you can help guide couples through this workbook and help them learn how to build a godly marriage.

As a mentor for premarried couples, you can help counter the years of poor training that many individuals have had. By allowing couples access to your lives and your marriage, allowing them to spend time with you and ask you questions, you can show these couples how a marriage between two imperfect people can work. They can observe firsthand what commitment to a godly, satisfying marriage relationship looks like.

The material in this course is formatted so that you become a facilitator, not a teacher. You don't need a seminary degree, and you don't need counseling experience. All you need is a desire to help guide the couples through the material, and then become a resource and friend. Your involvement in their lives may have a greater impact than anything else they learn in this course.

Format of the Workbook

Preparing for Marriage takes couples through a four-part interaction experience.

1. **"Preparing the Groundwork"** introduces couples to the workbook and then provides two worksheets for them to complete and discuss. "Understanding Your Personal History" includes dozens of questions designed to help each person understand the past and then discuss it as a couple. "Great Expectations" helps each person understand the expectations he or she is bringing into marriage. We recommend that couples complete and discuss these worksheet projects before continuing through the remainder of the workbook.

2. **"Laying the Foundation"** guides couples through the book of Genesis in two chapters that explore God's purposes and plans for marriage. This will be new information for many couples who know little about God's blueprint for making a marriage last a lifetime. Chapter 2 concludes with a bonus project: "Purity Covenant," which gives you the opportunity to challenge couples to maintain sexual purity until they are married.

3. **"Making the Decision"** challenges couples to take a hard and honest look at the strengths and weaknesses of their relationship and then make a decision about whether God is calling them together. In chapter 3, "Evaluating Your Relationship," couples discuss their relational and spiritual compatibility, examine different factors that can make it difficult for them to make a good decision and evaluate whether any serious issues need to be examined. Chapter 4, "A Decision-Making Guide" helps couples understand how to discern God's will for their future.

4. **"Building Oneness"** examines, in four final chapters, some key topics that couples need to discuss as they look at building a marriage that will last a lifetime.

The workbook concludes with a final challenge in "Where Do We Go from Here?" and two bonus projects: "Parental Wisdom Questionnaire" (appendix A) and "Couple Interview" (appendix B), which offers couples the opportunity to seek wisdom and guidance from their parents and from a married couple they respect.

Chapter Format

Each of the eight chapters includes several elements:

 True North—A statement of the biblical truth related to the topic of that chapter.

 Get the Picture—An introduction to the topic that gives couples the opportunity to answer questions and complete exercises that allow them to grasp the topic and understand why it is important.

Get the Truth—The Bible discovery section of each chapter in which they examine and discuss biblical truths to learn God's principles on different aspects of marriage.

 Navigating by True North: Truths to Chart Your Course—Summary statements of the key principles from each chapter.

 Couple's Project—The interaction portion of the session. Each project includes the following sections:

 Get Real: Questions to guide your discussion.

 Get to the Heart of Your Marriage: An opportunity to pray together and experience a spiritual discipline that will be one of the keys to a growing marriage in the years to come.

 Get Deeper: Optional assignments for the highly motivated—those who want to go where no engaged couple has gone before!

 Special Questions for Those Who Were Previously Married: We realize that many couples going through this workbook have been married before. These questions help them examine important issues unique to their experience.

Two other notes regarding format: First, in order to receive the most benefit from this notebook, we strongly recommend that each person obtain a workbook. Second, the word "fiancé(e)" has been chosen to represent both the man or woman, as in "meet with your fiancé(e) to discuss your answers." We realize this word may feel a bit strange, but we figure you'll be able to overlook that awkwardness as you work through this study.

Meeting with Couples

While a couple can complete the workbook on their own, their experience will be much more rewarding if they do it under the guidance of a pastor, counselor or mentor. This gives them the opportunity to learn from those who have gone through the same experiences and have built a solid marriage. It also gives you the opportunity to help couples make a solid, biblical decision about whether to marry; and understand key biblical truths to apply to their relationship as they begin marriage.

We have designed *Preparing for Marriage* so that you can use the material as you like: you can guide one couple at a time through the material or you can go through the chapters with several couples in a small group.

We have found that most mentors follow a simple plan for guiding couples through the material: *The couples complete and discuss assigned worksheets and chapters, and then they meet with mentors to further discuss the material.*

How many meetings should you schedule? That's up to you. But we encourage you to consider meeting at least five times with the couples you mentor. Below you will find a suggested sequence of meetings and topics to discuss.

While most couples who do receive premarriage counseling today only meet one or two times with a pastor or counselor, an increasing number of churches are recognizing the need for more extensive training.

Marriage Partnership magazine, in fact, once surveyed 3,000 couples, from 25 denominations, who had received premarital counseling. One question was, "Did your premarriage counseling help you in marriage?" The following is a breakdown of those who answered "definitely yes":

One counseling session received:	15 percent
Two sessions received:	31 percent
Five sessions received	53 percent
Seven or more sessions received:	75 percent

Suggested Sequences if You Meet 5 Times

First meeting
- ♥ Opening Interview (see pages 47-55)
- ♥ Assign couples to complete worksheets on "Understanding Your Personal History" and "Great Expectations."
- ♥ Assign couples to complete chapter 1 and chapter 2 before the next meeting.

Second meeting
- ♥ Discuss chapter 1 and chapter 2.
- ♥ Discuss "Understanding Your Personal History" worksheet.
- ♥ Assign couples to complete chapter 3 and chapter 4 before the next meeting.

Third meeting
- ♥ Discuss chapter 3 and chapter 4.
- ♥ Assign couples to complete chapter 5 and chapter 6 before the next meeting.

Fourth meeting
- ♥ Discuss chapter 5 and chapter 6.
- ♥ Discuss "Great Expectations" worksheet.
- ♥ Assign couples to complete chapter 7 and chapter 8 before the next meeting.

Fifth meeting
- ♥ Discuss chapter 7 and chapter 8.
- ♥ Discuss "Where Do We Go from Here?"

Suggested Sequences if You Meet 8 Times (Recommended)

First meeting	♥ Opening Interview (see pages 47-55)
	♥ Assign couples to complete worksheets on "Understanding Your Personal History" and "Great Expectations."
	♥ Assign couples to complete chapter 1 before the next meeting.

Second meeting	♥ Discuss chapter 1.
	♥ Discuss "Understanding Your Personal History" worksheet.
	♥ Assign couples to complete chapter 2 before the next meeting.

| Third meeting | ♥ Discuss chapter 2. |
| | ♥ Assign couples to complete chapter 3 and chapter 4 before the next meeting. |

| Fourth meeting | ♥ Discuss chapter 3 and chapter 4. |
| | ♥ Assign couples to complete chapter 5 before the next meeting. |

Fifth meeting	♥ Discuss chapter 5.
	♥ Discuss "Great Expectations" worksheet.
	♥ Assign couples to complete chapter 6 before the next meeting.

| Sixth meeting | ♥ Discuss chapter 6. |
| | ♥ Assign couples to complete chapter 7 before the next meeting. |

Seventh meeting:	♥ Discuss chapter 7.
	♥ Assign couples to complete chapter 8 before the next meeting.

Eighth meeting:	♥ Discuss chapter 8.
	♥ Discuss "Where Do We Go from Here?"

Small-Group Options

Some churches like to take groups of couples through the material. This can be a fun option for couples because they can interact with others going through the same experiences. There are a couple options for how this can work:

♥ The couples complete the worksheets and chapters on their own and then meet as a group with mentors to discuss the material.

♥ The couples complete the worksheets on their own but complete "Get the Picture" and "Get the Truth" sections of each chapter in the group meeting. Couples then complete the Couples Project at the end of each chapter before the next group meeting.

The suggested sequence for the small-group option remains the same as listed above.

Completing the *Preparing for Marriage* workbook with a mentor requires a high level of commitment from both the church and the premarried couple. The church should offer options that allow the couple to complete the workbook and mentoring sessions well in advance of a couple's wedding date. Couples, meanwhile, will need to plan an engagement long enough to incorporate so many weeks of training. We realize they may not be happy about completing such a long course, but if you do a good job of selling the advantages of this approach they should embrace it.

Tips for Leading a Small Group

1. Each chapter is designed for a time block of approximately 90 minutes. This would allow you 75 minutes for small-group discussion and 15 minutes for refreshments and fellowship. If you want to allow couples to work on their Couple's Project immediately after the small-group time, add another 30 minutes to your schedule.

   Once the people in your group get to know each other and interaction gets underway, you may find it more difficult to complete a session in the time allotted. You'll need to determine ahead of time which questions are most important to cover.

2. Each chapter combines teaching material and personal questions. As small-group leader, you could take on the role of *teacher* or *facilitator*, depending on which you prefer and how well you know the material.

   As teacher, you would present the material in "Get the Picture" and "Get the Truth" and weave in some personal stories of your own, but you'd still need to stop at each personal question for couples to answer in their group.

   As facilitator, you would cover the material in each chapter as you would a small-group Bible study. You'd read through sections of the text and stop for personal questions. Your goal would be to encourage couples to learn the material themselves as they look up Bible passages and discuss the different concepts. You will need to learn the material thoroughly so that you can keep the discussion on the right track and ensure that the couples are discerning the correct answers.

3. Do not let the sessions drag, become dull and boring or go on too long. Be sensitive to the needs of the group and gauge their attention span—when people stop contributing, they may have stopped listening as well. It is far better for people to wish the session could have gone on longer than for them to wish it had ended sooner. Keep it moving. Keep it lively.

4. Don't be afraid of a question that is greeted with group silence—some of the best answers come after moments of silent thought. Keep in mind as a group leader that 15 seconds can seem like 5 minutes.

5. If you find one or two particularly profound questions that you really want everyone to consider, think about having group members pause to consider the question individually and then write and share their answers with the group. Moments of silence and self-evaluation can be among the sharpest tools for truly teaching others. Use these moments strategically and sparingly.

6. Be sensitive to your use of time, and be careful not to make comments about time pressure, which will make the group feel rushed. When you need to move the discussion to the next item, say something like, "We could probably talk about that question the rest of the evening, but we need to consider several other important questions that bear on that issue."

7. You are the leader of your group and know the needs of the individual couples best. But keep in mind that the Holy Spirit will have an agenda for couples that you may never know about. "The mind of man plans his way, but the LORD directs his steps" (Prov. 16:9). Do your best to prepare and pray over the session, and then leave the results to God.

8. You will find many open-ended discussions throughout the study. One way to help stimulate discussion is to prepare some answers to these questions yourself. If you ask a question and nobody answers at first, give your own perspective and then open the discussion up to others.

Working with Couples Who Have Been Married Previously

When someone has been married before, he or she brings a new set of issues into a new marriage, especially if the first marriage ended in divorce. Most of the material in this study applies to previously married couples as much as it does to couples who have not been married. The bigger challenge, however, is getting them to discuss the more difficult topics such as analyzing the mistakes of the first marriage and coming to grips with the realities of a blended family.

Many of these issues will come to light in the special questions for previously married couples in the Couple's Project at the end of each session. You will want to look through the sessions and look for ways to adapt the material to the couple you are mentoring.

There are two key issues that couples who have been divorced need to face: First, *they need to admit their own responsibility for the failure of the marriage.* Many people want to put so much of the blame on the ex-spouse that they are unwilling to see their own failures.

Second, *they need to recognize the errors they made in the first marriage so they can trust God to change them and make it possible to build a better marriage this time around.* Otherwise they will repeat the same patterns that led to divorce in the first marriage.

One special note: Some of the questions are geared toward those who are divorced. If this is not the situation for the couple you are mentoring, lead them to those questions that will most apply to their situation.

Chapter 2

Ministering to Premarried Couples

Do you remember your own courtship and engagement? For many of us, it was an experience like no other—a time of great excitement and joy and romance and anticipation, but also a time of intense pressure and raw nerves.

As you look back upon this time now, however, you may be able to see it through different eyes. Were you caught up in the usual whirlwind of activities leading up to the wedding? Were you very well prepared for the marriage you were about to begin? Did you really know each other very well? Would you do anything differently now?

There are many engaged couples who are well prepared for marriage, but as you guide a couple through the workbook, you would be wise to assume that they don't realize what they don't know. They need your help to get them ready for the most important human relationship of their life on earth.

What to Remember About Premarried Couples

1. Many couples are *wearing blinders*. An engaged person is often aware of negative characteristics in the one he loves, but figures, "This will improve after we are married." Or he underestimates how self-centered he and his fiancé(e) are because both are suppressing their selfish behavior.

2. Many couples approach marriage with an *idealistic* view of how perfect everything will be. They do not foresee the normal problems and conflicts all couples face.

3. Because of the hectic schedule leading up to the wedding, reception and honeymoon, engaged couples are experiencing one of the most *stressful* times of their lives.

4. Many couples, whether they realize it or not, have demonstrated a *willingness to sacrifice some biblical values for the sake of the relationship*. A large number, for example, are already having sexual intercourse when they begin premarital counseling. A growing number are living together.

5. Those who are not having sexual intercourse are having difficulty keeping their sexual desires in check. They are *physically charged*, and it's difficult for them to draw boundaries and know when to stop.

6. Before most couples reach the altar, they usually experience a time of *financial pressure as a result of wedding expenses*. Everything seems to cost more than it should, or at least that's often what one person thinks.

7. Even though engaged couples have discussed many important topics during their courtship and engagement, many have talked very little about *normal financial habits and expenses*. As a result, they will often be surprised by the habits of their new spouse once they are married.

8. Many couples struggle with *extremes in emotions*. For some women, these emotions are amplified by reactions to birth control pills.

9. Many are so caught up in their excitement that they *fail to think rationally* about their future spouse. They pass over potential problems that could sabotage the relationship, thinking instead that "love conquers all."

10. They are *not acutely aware of their expectations* about the relationship and about marriage. As a result, they're setting themselves up for disappointment when reality sets in.

11. A significant number of couples have *discussed only in part how their past has affected them*. Many don't know about serious relational baggage they are bringing into the marriage.

12. Those who begin to have doubts about whether this marriage is right will feel *tremendous pressure to go ahead with the wedding* anyway. Some of this pressure will come from family members who have already made plans and spent money on the wedding. But much of the pressure is self-induced: They don't want to cause problems for their friends and family, or they don't want to be embarrassed by publicly admitting a failure. Women in their 30s may feel this is their "last chance" to find a spouse and begin a family.

And finally . . .

13. Many couples are *not excited about premarital counseling*. They consider it a necessary evil, just another thing they need to squeeze into an already busy schedule. They also think they already know it all anyway!

Goals in Ministering to Premarried Couples

Goal One: *Work to replace the idealized view of marriage with a more realistic view.* In his book *Communication: Key to Your Marriage*, H. Norman Wright says:

> Too many young couples enter marriage blinded by unrealistic expectations. They believe the relationship should be characterized by a high level of continuous romantic love. As one young adult said, "I wanted marriage to fulfill all my desires. I needed security, someone

to take care of me, intellectual stimulation, economic security immediately—but it just wasn't like that!" People are looking for something "magical" to happen in marriage.[1]

You don't want to destroy their idealism, but you do need to help them honestly evaluate their relationship. They need to see that the result of a lifelong commitment is that they will go through a lot of trials, problems and heartaches as well as joy and excitement.

Goal Two: *Help the couple come to an honest decision about whether God is really calling them together.* During the course of this study, couples may learn more about each other than they ever dreamed possible. And yet even then they'll barely scratch the surface! Your job will be to guide them through the process and encourage them to be open to God's leading. Encourage them to take their time and not feel pressured to get engaged or married.

The workbook is *designed to bring difficult questions, doubts or qualms to the surface.* Ask questions that leave couples uneasy, forcing them to honestly determine whether this is God's will for them. Too many couples fail to ask the tough questions this workbook will raise, and later on they pay the price for this failure.

Goal Three: *Give them a glimpse of your own marriage relationship.* This is especially important if you work with someone who comes from a broken home. This individual may never have seen a marriage work the way it should; your relationship may be the first biblically based model he or she has observed. As you work with an engaged couple, spend time with them apart from your scheduled meetings. Invite them over for dinner or go out with them on a double date. Let them see how you relate to your spouse and to your children.

Give them the freedom to ask you tough questions. Share your mistakes as well as your triumphs. Tell them how you've resolved conflict, how you've made decisions together and how you've faced various types of trials.

Goal Four: *Hold them accountable.* Accountability is a scriptural principle that tells us to "be subject to one another in the fear of Christ" (Eph. 5:21). This means choosing to submit your life to the scrutiny of another person to gain spiritual strength, growth and balance.

Accountability means asking the other person for advice. It means giving the other person the freedom to make honest observations and evaluations about you. It means remaining teachable and approachable.

Accountability is a key ingredient of this course, and you must establish it at the very beginning. You can do this in two ways.

First, let the couple know what is expected of them, and follow through each time you meet to see if they've completed their assignments. Emphasize the importance of completing the homework assigned each session. If you see the couple consistently coming to the session with incomplete homework, note it as a danger signal and set up an individual session with them to discuss any potential problems. Also, you'll need to determine ahead of time how many sessions you will allow a couple to miss and how they can make up sessions they miss.

Second, let them know from the beginning that they are free to ask you about anything, and that you will take the freedom to *ask them* about anything. As you work with the couple, different issues will undoubtedly surface. It's important for you to hold them accountable to discuss and resolve these issues as much as possible. For example, if you discover that one person wants to have a large family but the other is hesitant to even have a child, you need to hold them accountable to work through that issue before they are married. Ask them if they've discussed it and what decisions they've made.

Your accountability also will help couples maintain sexual purity before marriage. Don't be afraid to ask them if they've been able to keep their hands off each other!

Goal Five: *Encourage them to walk closely with Christ.* As followers of Christ, our purpose in life is to know God and to glorify Him with our lives. The power to live wisely and walk with righteousness comes from our relationship with God—and that means that the power to create a lasting marriage comes from Him. Throughout the workbook you have the opportunity to encourage them to walk in obedience to God and His Word.

One of the greatest tests of faith for many premarried couples comes in their preparation for marriage, especially in the areas of sexual purity and cohabitation. It is safe to say that these will be major issues for every couple you mentor; even those who are not sleeping together are facing temptation every day.

If you discover that a couple is sleeping together or living together, it's important to talk it over with them and challenge them to trust God with their lives. And it's important for you to discern the depth of their faith and spiritual commitment. If a couple is continually disobeying God in this area, this reveals that they are spiritually immature at best. It also may reveal that they are not truly followers of Christ at all. Encourage them to commit their lives to Christ and accept His forgiveness for their sins. In many cases, it would be wise to encourage them to postpone wedding plans while they focus on growing in their faith.

Suggested Tools and Resources

Personality/Temperament Tests
Two popular tests for premarriage counseling are:

1. Taylor-Johnson Temperament Analysis; Psychological Publications, Inc. (www.tjta.com)

2. Prepare-Enrich couple assessment; Life Innovations (www.prepare-enrich.com)

Both of these websites offer the opportunity to take the test online.

Recommended Books on Marriage and Premarriage:

Staying Close, by Dennis and Barbara Rainey, Word Publishing, 1989

Before You Say I Do, by Wes Roberts and H. Norman Wright, 1997

Communication: Key to Your Marriage, by H. Norman Wright, Regal Books, 2000

Intended for Pleasure, by Ed and Gail Wheat, Fleming H. Revell Co., 1981

Master Your Money, by Ron Blue, Thomas Nelson Inc., 1993

Passion and Purity, by Elisabeth Elliot, Fleming H. Revell Co., 2002

Love and Respect, by Emerson Eggerichs, Thomas Nelson, 2004

Rocking the Roles, by Robert Lewis and William D. Hendricks, 1999

Moments Together for Couples, by Dennis and Barbara Rainey, Regal Books, 1995

Moments with You, by Dennis and Barbara Rainey, Regal Books, 2007

Complete Financial Guide for Young Couples, by Larry Burkett, David C. Cook, 2002

Marriage Conference

We recommend all couples try to attend a Weekend to Remember marriage conference in the city nearest them or the conference closest to their anticipated wedding date in order to be fully equipped with God's blueprint for marriage. For more information, call 1-800-FL-TODAY or look for information at www.familylife.com.

Note

1. H. Norman Wright, *Communication: Key to Your Marriage* (Ventura, CA: Regal Books, 2000), introduction.

Chapter 3

Using Mentors

In many churches, pastors handle all the premarried counseling. But one of the most significant trends of the church today is equipping lay people to be involved in mentoring.

Recently, FamilyLife hired a professional to help us form focus groups that would help us learn how we could better strengthen families. The results of the research were startling. We asked people what they wanted to make their marriages and families successful. One by one they all said pretty much the same thing: They wanted a mentor, someone who had already been through his or her phase of life and could guide them.

They wanted a real, live person of whom they could ask questions—questions about resolving conflicts, about babies sleeping through the night, about romance and sex after you start having children, about balancing the demands of work and family.

The same goes for premarried couples. Many have no idea how to make a marriage work, because they've never seen one modeled. They come from broken or dysfunctional homes, and they are afraid they will repeat the same pattern.

In the midst of the crisis that swirls around family issues, churches are sitting on an untapped gold mine of married couples who could act as mentors. These couples—especially those who have been married for more than 15 years—need to be challenged to pour their lives into younger couples—both married and premarried. But many of these couples lack confidence—they feel they have nothing to offer. They need a passionate challenge and a little training.

Mentoring couples can take a load off of a pastor and make the premarriage counseling ministry one of the most dynamic in the church. Yes, there will be some situations that mentoring couples will not be equipped to handle. But we've found that a large majority of premarried couples benefit tremendously from exposure to a mentoring couple who can guide them through the workbook.

Finding Mentoring Couples

Look around your church. Who comes to mind when you think of healthy Christian marriages? Is there anyone who has a desire to help reach other families? Who has the ability to relate to younger couples and remember what it was like to be in their shoes, before and after marriage? Who has experience in leading small groups?

Here are some specifics of what to look for:

- People with the spiritual gifts of exhortation, encouragement, discernment, teaching or shepherding
- Couples with a desire to help others learn what has worked for them
- People with a passion for the Lord and an ability to live out biblical principles in their lives and in their marriages
- Couples who have been married five years or more, especially couples whose children are grown, and who have the desire and ability to minister to younger couples
- Couples who demonstrate that their own marriages are growing relationships
- Couples who are willing to acknowledge their own struggles as well as their successes

♥ People with good interpersonal skills and initiative and who have the willingness and the time to build friendships with young couples
♥ People with a willingness to lovingly confront and discuss sometimes-difficult issues pertaining to marriage

After you have recruited some mentor couples, and prior to beginning the course, meet with them and discuss the following:

♥ The importance of their role
♥ The difference between a "lecture approach" and a "facilitator approach" (Couples who have gone through premarital counseling have asked that the content be interactive. They need time to talk it out with the leaders, each other and other couples facing the same new adventure of marriage. So the role of the mentoring couple during small-group interaction is one of discussion leader rather than teacher.)
♥ The subject matter. Give them each a copy of the workbook, and quickly go through it to explain the format and the content.
♥ How the personality testing will be handled
♥ Who will conduct the opening interview
♥ Up-to-date information on church wedding policies
♥ When any needed training and information about working with premarried couples will be available
♥ What preparation they need in handling delicate issues such as divorce, sexual intimacy, concerns about the relationship, and so on. Discuss when they need to talk to you about problems that might surface.
♥ Any books or articles you would recommend to prepare for their role

Do not overwhelm these mentoring couples. Sort out and prepare what you think is the most important preparation for them.

As a leader, you will serve these mentoring couples well if you monitor their progress by doing the following:

- ♥ Sit in on one of their sessions if you can.
- ♥ Give them positive and constructive feedback.
- ♥ Talk with them regularly.
- ♥ Encourage them further in their own marriage.

Ministry Opportunity Description for Mentoring Couples

Position
Mentoring couple for "Preparing for Marriage" course.

Description
Lead a small group of three to four couples during a course for engaged and pre-engaged couples. Meet with couples for counseling and informal times outside the sessions. Model your relationship to them.

Spiritual Gifts
Exhortation, encouragement, discernment, teaching, shepherding.

Requirements
1. Married five years or more.
2. Must demonstrate a growing marriage relationship.
3. Both spouses must be involved.
4. Basic biblical and theological understanding of marriage.
5. Willingness to acknowledge problems as well as successes in marriage.
6. Willingness to build friendships with couples; good interpersonal skills and ability to take initiative.
7. Willingness to lovingly confront and discuss sometimes difficult issues pertaining to marriage.
8. Participation in previous small groups, and a good working knowledge of how they work.

Commitment
1. Prepare well to facilitate each of the eight sessions.
2. Should not miss more than one time.
3. Meet at least three times privately with each couple during the eight-session course.

Benefits
1. Provides an opportunity to make a big impact in the lives of others.
2. Strengthens your own marriage.
3. Reduces counseling load for pastors and counselors.
4. Demystifies Christian marriages. Premarrieds desperately need to see models of healthy Christian marriages.
5. Serves as ongoing, viable line to the local church for friendship and future counsel to the newlyweds.
6. Reduces the divorce rate!

Chapter 4

Conducting the Opening Interview

General Comments

1. We highly recommend starting your premarriage counseling with an opening interview with the premarried couple. This accomplishes several goals:

   ♥ It gives you the opportunity to begin developing a relationship with the couple.
   ♥ It helps you learn more about them and how they have reached this point in their relationship.
   ♥ It lets them know about the workbook and its requirements.
   ♥ It helps you determine if the couple is ready to begin premarriage counseling.

2. The opening interview is divided into two sections: "Personal Questions" and "Course Overview." You should complete this interview with the couple before they begin the chapters in the workbook. *Do not give a copy of the interview to the couple; it is designed for you to ask the questions verbally and make note of their answers.* You have permission to photocopy the interview pages for each time you do an opening interview.

3. As previously stated, there are four goals to this interview:

   ♥ To give you the opportunity to begin developing a
     relationship with the couple.
   ♥ To learn more about the couple and how they have
     reached this point in their relationship.
   ♥ To let the couple know about the course and its re-
     quirements.
   ♥ To determine whether the couple is ready to begin
     the course.

   The fourth goal—determining if the couple is ready
   for premarriage counseling—is a difficult one to quantify.
   While conducting the interview, you may begin to develop some serious doubts about whether this couple is
   making a wise decision about moving toward marriage.
   Don't break in immediately and begin counseling or ex-
   horting; continue the questions and let the couple continue to talk and build trust in you. Instead, take
   advantage of the changes of subject during the Personal
   Questions to sensitively inject some personal questions
   or comments.

4. We suggest setting aside at least two hours for this interview to allow enough time for the couple to answer the
   questions and for you to develop a relationship. You could
   include lunch or dinner in the first part of your meeting,
   but do not ask the questions in the section on Moral
   Guidelines while in a public place.

5. Begin the interview by telling them a little about yourself, your marriage and your family. Commend them for
   taking the time to evaluate their potential marriage.
   Then begin the questions in section one, "History of the
   Relationship."

Personal Questions

1. The questions in "History of the Relationship" give you the opportunity to evaluate the depth and strength of the couple's relationship. As they describe how they met and how their relationship developed, your job is to listen and draw them out. Jot down notes about the strengths and weaknesses you perceive in the relationship. Also listen for comments that may indicate potential problems, and be sure to address these areas in the future.

2. "Spiritual History" will help you evaluate each person's spiritual beliefs and convictions. Be sure to encourage both people to talk so you can see if one person seems much more mature in this area than the other.

   If, after completing this section, you are concerned that one or both individuals may not be Christians, this would be a good opportunity for you to explain the plan of salvation. You might also sense that they are young or immature in their faith. In either case, recommend that the couple complete a study on the fundamentals of the Christian faith with you or with someone else in the church. Also, ask them to wait at least six months before pursuing any wedding plans. Explain the benefits to them: As they learn more about how to build a relationship with God, the foundation of their potential union will only become stronger (see Matt. 7:24-27).

3. The section on "Moral Guidelines" explores a sensitive area, because many premarried couples are either sleeping together or, if they are not, have very loose boundaries about their sexual behavior. An increasing number of couples are cohabiting before marriage. This is an important issue, because it reveals the maturity of each individual's faith and the strength of their relationship. In most cases, we encourage you to take this opportunity to strongly challenge the couple in this area, because we feel that sexual involvement

before marriage not only violates God's commandments but also prevents them from making a clear decision about how He is leading in their relationship.

This is the first of your opportunities to challenge couples in this area; the subject also comes up in chapter 2. (*Important note: Be sure to avoid asking these questions in a public place, where couples will probably feel reluctant to discuss personal matters.*)

Watch each person closely as you discuss the following issue, and especially as you ask about his or her physical involvement. You may catch some people off guard when you ask them this question, and their reaction may be revealing. Others may anticipate the fact that you will ask them about sex, and may not answer truthfully. Do not hesitate to ask about specifics as they respond.

When this subject is discussed again in chapter 2, couples are given the opportunity to sign a "Purity Covenant" located at the end of the Couples Project in that chapter. They look closely at God's desire for them to be sexually pure before marriage and they sign a commitment to do so until their honeymoon. Depending on the circumstances and the openness of your conversation with the couple, you could point out this covenant and have them sign it before your next meeting rather than waiting until later.

We do *not* recommend waiting until the end of the study to challenge a couple in this area. Whether you do it during the opening interview or when you discuss chapter 2, this is an issue that needs to be confronted clearly, honestly and near the beginning of the sessions.

Course Overview

1. In this section of the opening interview, you tell them about the workbook and how you will use it. You will give them a schedule of when they will meet with you. You will discuss

the goals of the workbook and explain the concept of mentoring. If one or both of them has been married previously, tell them that most of the principles in the workbook will apply to them just as they would to any other premarried couple. They do, however, have additional special questions located at the end of the Couple's Projects that will help them discuss some key areas of their relationship.

2. When you reach the section on format, give them a copy of the workbook. Show them how the workbook is put together, and explain each part—the worksheets, the main chapters, the Couple's Projects. Set up the next date when you will meet.

3. As you explain the course format, be sure to encourage the couple to complete the first two worksheets on "Understanding Your Personal History" and "Great Expectations" before they begin the chapters.

4. Explain that the course requires a high degree of effort and accountability. They should, however, enjoy the experience as much as they benefit from it. Ask the couple if they feel they can make the commitment to this study. If they hesitate because of a busy schedule, find out what commitments they are facing currently. Talk through these, and challenge them to set aside some other responsibilities, if necessary, to make this study a priority.

5. If you have a church policy on setting a wedding date, let them know it. If you do not currently have a policy, here's our recommendation: State that, because marriage is such a serious proposition, you need to reserve the right to recommend that they postpone a wedding if necessary. Tell them that they are free to set a date, but that they should set it far enough in advance that they could easily postpone the wedding if issues arise during the course that

lead you to conclude they need more time before they marry. A common "point of no return" in the minds of many couples is the date when wedding invitations are mailed. If a couple sets a date for at least two months after the end of the course, that would allow them enough time to postpone the date if necessary before they'd need to send out the invitations.

6. Encourage couples to attend a Weekend to Remember conference to learn even more about building a solid marriage that will last a lifetime. Give the couple a brochure for the conference or show them the website where they can get more information. You can obtain current brochures from FamilyLife by calling 1-800-FLTODAY.

Additional Tips

1. If your spouse will be involved with you in this mentoring relationship, conduct the initial interview together.

2. Many premarried couples will feel nervous about this initial meeting. Look for ways to get them feeling relaxed so they can be honest with their answers.

3. Adjust your comments depending on whether the couple is engaged or not.

4. Explain your role, letting the couple know that you have their best interests and the success of their future marriage at heart. You want them to win, which is why from time to time you will be evaluating their responses to one another and possibly sharing some difficult information with them.

Opening Interview

INTERVIEWER

NAME: _____ Date: _____

PERSONAL INFORMATION

NAME: _____ AGE: _____

Street Address
_____

City _____ State _____ Zip _____

Phone (home) _____ (office) _____
(cell) _____

Vocation _____

NAME: _____ AGE: _____

Street Address
_____

City _____ State _____ Zip _____

Phone (home) _____ (office) _____
(cell) _____

Vocation _____

Are you engaged?   ❑ Yes   ❑ No

If so, what is your anticipated wedding date? _____

Personal Questions

History of the Relationship

1. How did you meet? How long have you been dating each other?

   _____

   _____

   _____

   _____

   _____

2. What kinds of dates have you had (types of activities; whether they primarily spent time just with themselves or with other people, and so on)?

   _____

   _____

   _____

   _____

   _____

3. Briefly tell about your families.

   _____

   _____

   _____

   _____

   _____

   Are your parents still alive? _____

   Do you have brothers or sisters? If so, how many?
   Brothers _____
   Sisters _____

   Are any of your brothers or sisters already married?
   ❏ Yes ❏ No

4. How would you evaluate your parents' marriage?

_____

_____

_____

_____

_____

5. How well have you gotten to know each other's family?

_____

_____

_____

_____

_____

6. How do your family and friends feel about your relationship?

_____

_____

_____

_____

_____

7. Have you ever broken off your relationship?

   If so, why did this happen?

_____

_____

_____

_____

   Why did you get back together?

_____

_____

_____

_____

8. Why did you decide to marry each other? OR: Why are you considering marriage?

_____

_____

_____

_____

_____

9. Why do you think this marriage will work?

_____

_____

_____

_____

_____

10. What preparation for marriage have you had?

_____

_____

_____

_____

_____

11. What would you hope to receive from this premarriage workbook and counseling?

_____

_____

_____

_____

_____

12. Are there any concerns or problems that you feel need to be addressed in your relationship?

_____

_____

_____

_____

13. Is there anything that you would like to ask or share that we haven't discussed?

_____

_____

_____

_____

_____

14. Have you been married before? _____

If so, were you widowed or divorced? _____

If you were divorced:

♥ How did it end?

_____

_____

_____

_____

_____

♥ When was your divorce finalized?

_____

♥ Has your previous spouse remarried?

_____

♥ Can you identify any failings that contributed to the breakdown of your previous marriage?

_____

_____

_____

_____

_____

♥ What have you done to resolve those issues?

_____

_____

_____

_____

_____

♥ Do you have any children from this previous marriage?

_____

♥ What living arrangement has been determined for the children?

_____

_____

_____

_____

_____

♥ Is that a good working relationship for all parties concerned? Why or why not?

_____

_____

_____

_____

_____

Spiritual Background

1. Tell me about your church and spiritual background.

_____

_____

_____

_____

2. This church is committed to building strong marriages
   with Christ at the center. Why do you think Jesus Christ
   came to earth?

   _____

   _____

   _____

   _____

   _____

   _____

3. What effect has Jesus Christ had on your life?

   _____

   _____

   _____

   _____

   _____

   _____

   Where is Jesus Christ in relationship to you?

   _____

   _____

   _____

   _____

   _____

   _____

   Is He your personal Savior and Lord?

   _____

4. What part has God played in your relationship?

   _____

   _____

   _____

   _____

   _____

   _____

5. What part do you expect God to play in your marriage?

Moral Guidelines

Note: Be sure NOT to discuss these
questions in a public place.

1. As couples grow closer to each other emotionally and spiritually, a natural response is to move closer to each other
   physically. God intends this area of our lives to be enjoyed
   to the fullest, but within the context of marriage (see Heb.
   13:4; 1 Thess. 4:3-8). In fact, we devote an entire session of
   the course to this topic. Why do you think God would design sex to be enjoyed only within the context of marriage?
   Do you see any benefits to waiting?

---

2. Because the Scriptures are our authority and blueprint,
   because we care about you, and because of the normal
   sexual pressures you face, we will ask you at different
   times in the weeks ahead how you are doing in this area.
   We sincerely want to see you win and build a strong foun-

dation from the start in your marriage. How do you feel about this?

_____

_____

_____

_____

_____

3. Can you tell me what your physical involvement with each other has been up to this point?

_____

_____

_____

_____

_____

What are your boundaries?

_____

_____

_____

_____

_____

4. Are you willing to abstain from sexual involvement until your marriage?

_____

Overview of *Preparing for Marriage*

> **Note:** The information on these pages is not to be given to the premarried couple. Explain it to them either by reading it or telling them.

Goals
We desire that each participant:

* Be exposed to the important building blocks for a healthy Christian marriage.
* Know what a Christian marriage looks like.
* Develop the skills to lay a good foundation from the beginning.
* Know how to evaluate whether God would have you marry each other, and whether this is the right time to marry.

Significance
We consider this a critical study that will help you lay a solid foundation for marriage. If you really love this person that you are considering marrying, the time you put into this study will demonstrate how much you care and how much you want what God desires in a marriage.

Format
1. The *Preparing for Marriage* workbook begins with two worksheets for you to complete: "Understanding Your Personal History" and "Great Expectations."

2. These are followed by eight chapters on the following topics:

   ♥ Why Marriage?
   ♥ God's Equation for Marriage: When One Plus One
      Equals One
   ♥ Evaluating Your Relationship
   ♥ A Decision-Making Guide
   ♥ Authentic Communication
   ♥ Roles and Responsibilities
   ♥ Money, Money, Money
   ♥ Intimacy: Sexual Communication in Marriage

3. The workbook also offers two bonus projects: the "Parental Wisdom Questionnaire" (appendix A), which gives your parents the opportunity to give you input about marriage, and the "Couple Interview" (appendix B), where you talk with a couple about building a marriage that lasts.

4. Each chapter ends with a Couple's Project. These will take about 90 minutes (sometimes longer) to complete with your fiancé(e).

Schedule
Explain how often you will meet with the couple (see suggestions on pages 21-23), and set up your next appointment.

About Mentoring Couples
Explain that the purpose of premarriage mentoring is to let couples interact with another couple so they can observe a marriage, ask questions and listen to honest reflections of that couple's successes and failures. These mentoring couples, who have been trained and screened by the church, will be friends and resources to help the couple in the future.

Church Wedding Policies
Explain any church wedding policies, if applicable.

Interview Summary

(To be completed after the meeting.)

1. What were your overall impressions of this couple?

   _____

   _____

   _____

   _____

   _____

2. What level of emotional maturity does each person bring to this relationship?

   _____

   _____

   _____

   _____

   _____

3. What level of spiritual maturity do you see in each person?

   _____

   _____

   _____

   _____

   _____

   _____

4. What strengths do they exhibit that will help their relationship?

   _____

   _____

   _____

   _____

5. What concerns/red flags need to be explored and addressed further?

_____

_____

_____

_____

_____

_____

6. Were they informed of church wedding policies?
   ☐ Yes   ☐ No

7. Did you explain the gospel with them?
   ☐ Yes   ☐ No

8. Other comments:

_____

_____

_____

_____

_____

_____

_____

_____

_____

_____

_____

_____

_____

_____

_____

_____

_____

_____

Chapter 5

Notes on the Couple's Workbook

In this chapter we offer comments and suggestions about each section and chapter of the workbook, in the order they appear. For most we include suggestions of things for you to discuss with the couple as their mentor.

As we mentioned in the previous chapter, most mentors meet with couples and discuss the different topics after the couples have completed chapters on their own. For each chapter, and for the two opening worksheets of the workbook, you will find a suggested sequence of questions you can ask during your discussion.

If you are leading a couple or a small group through the workbook without having them complete it first, we assume you will ask all of the questions in the workbook in order. If you use this format, however, we highly recommend that couples complete chapters 3 and 4 by themselves before discussing them with you.

Finally, if you are counseling a couple where one or both people were married previously, be sure to ask them how they answered the special questions at the end of each chapter's Couple's Project.

Worksheet 1

Understanding Your Personal History

General Comments

1. Although premarried couples know a lot about each other, this worksheet will help them learn a lot more. It also will help alert all of you to any potential problems arising from the past. Most premarried couples don't realize what they don't know about marriage. They also have no clue how problems from the past will affect their marriage.

   For example, an increasing number of young people marrying today grew up in homes torn apart by divorce. They observed a marriage fail, and many may have never observed a marriage relationship that worked properly. Unless they take an honest look at the past and determine how it has affected them, they may be unable to prevent themselves from following the same path.

2. Some Christians may deny the influence of the past, citing 2 Corinthians 5:17, which tells us we are new creatures in Christ. It's true that we have been forgiven, and it's true that God gives us the power to grow more like Christ. Our new life in Christ, however, does not mean that the scars of the past disappear. There are consequences to the choices we make, both good and bad. Also, there are consequences to the choices our parents made.

3. We suggest that couples fill out the worksheet individually, and then meet together to share their answers. At some point during your personal meetings with them, you should discuss the worksheet. You probably don't have time to go through the entire worksheet with them, and a few of the questions also appear in the Opening Interview, so here is a suggested sequence for your discussion:

   a. Ask, "What did you think of the 'Understanding Your Personal History' worksheet?"
   b. Ask, "What were some of the most interesting or important things you've learned about each other?"
   c. In "Section One: Your Relationship History," ask how they answered questions 2 and 4.
   d. In "Section Two: Your Family," ask how they answered the questions under "Home Environment" and "Parents."
   e. In "Section Three: Your Spiritual Journey," ask how they answered questions 1 and 4.

   Be on the alert for any major issues that may come up during your discussion. If the woman mentions, for example, that her father deserted the family when she was a young girl, you will want to discuss this situation more thoroughly, either now or in the future.

4. *Sharing as a mentor:* Take a few minutes to read through the Understanding Your Personal History worksheet, and find some examples to share of issues about your own past that you wish you had discussed before you were married. Perhaps you and your wife came from very different family environments—socially, economically, relationally, and so on. Talk about what you didn't know before you were married, and how learning about your backgrounds helped you in specific ways.

5. If you have the opportunity to talk individually to each person, ask if it was difficult to talk about the past, and why. Ask if there was anything about the past that he or she was reluctant to share.

Worksheet 2

Great Expectations

General Comments

1. Each of us brings expectations into a relationship. Many of our expectations are neither good nor bad, but trouble develops when they conflict with those of your spouse. Unresolved expectations often lead to demands, and demands lead to manipulation and conflict.

    Most premarried couples have thought very little about expectations. Then, they often spend years uncovering the expectations they bring into a marriage. This worksheet has two purposes: to uncover some of those expectations and to alert couples to the need to discuss them.

2. Discussing the worksheet with the couple will also give you the opportunity to address the expectations they express and also discuss common unrealistic expectations that couples bring into marriage. Couples need to understand:

    ♥ The intense feelings of love and passion they experience now will fade some after marriage—but these feelings can often be rekindled if we make romance a priority.

    ♥ Life will not always be as exciting after marriage as it is when they are engaged.

    ♥ Marriage is not always a cure for loneliness.

- Even though God brings two people together who will complete each other (this is one of the topics discussed in chapter 1), they will not meet *all* of each other's needs. There are other needs that only other people can fill, and others that only God can fill.

- They should not get married with the idea of making their spouse a better person. This often happens, but it just as often does not.

- They will experience periods of conflict and difficulties, and part of the joy of marriage is working through those times.

- Marrying a Christian is not the *final* step to building a lasting marriage; it is only the beginning. That's why marrying someone who is *consistently and humbly walking before God* should be the more important criteria.

3. We placed this worksheet at the beginning of the workbook so that couples can complete it before beginning the main chapters. We suggest discussing it in an early meeting (see pages 21-23).

4. Following is a suggested sequence for discussing this worksheet:

    a. Ask, "Have you ever discussed this subject of expectations?"
    b. Ask how they answered the questions under the heading "Illusion and Reality."
    c. Ask if they discussed their expectations survey together, and whether they were able to apply the suggestions listed under "A Guiding Principle" and "Discussing Expectations."
    d. In the Expectations Survey, ask how they answered the following questions:

- Question 1 under "Marriage Relationship"
- Questions 1-7 under "Finances" (another option is to save these questions for when you meet with the couple after chapter 7 on finances)
- Questions 3 and 4 under "Home"
- Questions 1 through 4 under "Housekeeping"
- Questions 1 and 2 under "Children and Parenting"
- Questions 1 and 2 under "Spiritual"
- Question 1 under "Holidays/Vacations/Special Occasions"
- Question 5 under "Parents/Relatives"
- Questions 1 and 2 under "Sex" (another option would be to save these questions for when you meet with the couple after chapter 8 on intimacy)

5. *Sharing as a mentor:* As you did with the Understanding Your Personal History worksheet, look through the questions and think of some specific expectations you brought into marriage that were not discussed before the wedding. For example, you may have begun your marriage with the expectation that you would spend Christmas with your parents every year, and then discovered your spouse expected to spend the holidays with his or her parents. Talk about how you resolved—or didn't resolve—that difference.

Session 1

Why Marriage?

General Comments

1. Most couples today have little idea what the Bible says about building a marriage and family. This chapter and the following one present God's blueprint for marriage through an intense examination of Genesis 1 and 2. By the end of chapter 1, couples should see that marriage is a much more important institution than they may have dreamed. At its core, marriage is a spiritual relationship between a man, a woman and the Lord God. Chapter 2 then builds upon this idea by presenting God's plan for oneness.

2. The first two chapters lead the couple steadily to the realization that, in order to build a solid marriage, they need to take their marriage vows seriously. They need to receive each other as God's provision and make a lifelong commitment to oneness. If they are unable to make such a commitment to each other, they should cancel or postpone their wedding plans.

3. The section, "Get the Picture," begins the story of Eric and Amanda and their road to a oneness marriage. Case studies like this allow couples the freedom to discuss and learn from a hypothetical situation and not feel threatened even when the fictional relationship is very similar to their own.

The story in this section highlights how Eric and Amanda met and decided to marry. The story is typical in many ways because so many couples begin marriage with little idea of how to make it work.

4. "Get the Truth" discusses three purposes for marriage as outlined in the book of Genesis:

   a. *To mutually complete one another:* Many premarried couples will be able to grasp this concept because they're aware of many of their differences and they probably see those differences in a positive light. After marriage they may look at things differently, and it's sometimes a revelation for couples who have been married five years or more to think of how they really do complete each other in a more profound way than they had ever realized.

   b. *To multiply a godly legacy:* While most couples want to start a family, a significant number marry with no intention of having children. Some say they want to focus on building their careers, while others believe they would not make good parents. These couples need to be challenged with the fact that the Bible does not make childbearing an option. Some couples are unable to have children, but those who can need to take some time to weigh their desires in light of God's Word.

   Most couples who do want children have given little thought to the critical importance of parenting in God's plan. This chapter could lead to some discussions about when they want to begin a family and about their philosophies of parenting.

   c. *To mirror God's image:* This is often the most difficult for couples to grasp. The final paragraph just before question 10 is critical: "When people look at your marriage, what will they see? Two people using each other to meet their own needs and experiencing nothing but conflict because of their selfishness? Or two imperfect people determined to love each other unconditionally and reaching out to others with the overflow of that love? In a time when about 50 percent of marriages eventually end in divorce, a successful marriage becomes a testimony of God's love and power."

5. Since this is the first chapter, and since much of this information may be new to each couple, don't press too hard about how they are going to apply these principles in their relationship. You'll have the opportunity to give them a stronger challenge during the next chapter.

6. *Sharing as a mentor:* When discussing how God brings together a man and woman to complete one another, tell the couple some of the different ways that you and your spouse fill each other's gaps. Tell them some of the things that you continue to learn about this even after years of marriage.

    If you have children, during the section on leaving a godly legacy, talk about some of your goals as a parent. Tell them about what you've done to help your children grow up to know and love the Lord.

    The section on mirroring God's image will become clearer to couples if you are able to give them an example of how you have seen part of God's character revealed in the marriage of your own parents or of someone you know.

7. Suggested sequence:

    a. Ask, "What were some things that you learned about God's purposes for marriage as you completed this chapter?"

b. Ask, "What did you learn about yourself during this chapter?"

c. Ask, "What did you learn about your fiancé(e) during this chapter?"

d. In "Get the Picture," ask how they answered question 2.

e. In "Get the Truth," ask how they answered questions 1, 5, 6, 7 and 10.

f. In the Couple's Project, ask how they answered question 3. Also, if someone has been previously married, discuss all the questions in "Special Questions for Those Who Were Previously Married."

Session 2

God's Equation
for Marriage:
When One Plus One Equals One

General Comments

1. This chapter builds upon the truths presented in chapter 1. Continuing the Genesis story, it presents God's plan for marriage.

2. In "Get the Picture," the story of Eric and Amanda continues with some troubles they experience after they are married. These struggles highlight the problem of incompatibility, which undermines many marriages. This leads directly to the themes discussed in the remainder of the chapter.

3. "Get the Truth" then presents God's plan for marriage—four key commitments that are critical for premarried couples to make in order to build a oneness marriage:

    ♥ *Commitment Number One: Receive Your Spouse.* This requires the ability to see that, if God has given you a spouse, this person is His provision for your needs. In the previous chapter the couples examined their respective strengths and weaknesses and how they complemented one another. They need to understand that they cannot enter marriage with the idea of changing the other person to meet their idealized version of a spouse.

♥ *Commitment Number Two: Leave Your Parents.* The concept of leaving one's parents is important because, when you marry, your spouse becomes more important. Leaving one's parents doesn't mean abandoning them or breaking off the relationship; it just means that your marriage relationship has a higher priority that will sometimes lead to some difficult choices.

There are many ways that newly married couples fail to leave their parents. They fail to leave *financially* by remaining dependent upon their parents for money. They fail to leave *emotionally* by remaining more attached to them than to their spouses. In some cases, they fail to leave *physically* by living so close to them and seeing them so often that they undermine their new priority of making their marriage relationship work.

Leaving one's parents is especially difficult when the parents won't let go. Before a child is married, the wise parent will think through this issue and meet with the child to discuss how their relationship will change.

♥ *Commitment Number Three: Cleave to Your Mate.* Many couples today begin marriage with the idea that, if it doesn't work, they can always get a divorce and try again. In fact, some marriage "experts" even claim that this process is healthy because couples can "learn from their mistakes" and build a better marriage the second time around.

The Scriptures make it clear, however, that God hates divorce. When two people are married, they take a sacred vow—a covenant between them and the Lord—and He takes that covenant seriously.

By establishing the marriage relationship as a covenant, God sets it apart from every other relationship. From this new union a new family is formed. He designed marriage as a monogamous relationship with a member of the opposite sex, because He knew that for this relationship to work both people needed to be able to totally trust each other. You can't trust another person who may bail out when the relationship becomes difficult.

♥ *Commitment Number Four: Become One Flesh.* Many singles believe that sex is merely a way of expressing love, of getting to know one another. But God designed sexual intimacy with much more in mind. It is the final point in the bonding process. It is designed to follow commitment in marriage, not precede it.

4. "Get the Truth" ends with a key section titled, "The Heart of a Oneness Marriage." Everything in chapters 1 and 2 lead to these few paragraphs, which summarize God's blueprint for marriage and challenge the couple to answer two key questions before they move toward marriage: "Is Christ at the center of your life?" and "Is God calling you together as man and wife?"

Since marriage is, at its heart, an intensely spiritual relationship between a man, a woman and God, you should be comfortable with how the couple answers these questions before you counsel them to marry. If Christ is not at the center of both of their lives, they will not be able to build their home on a solid spiritual foundation. And if they do not have a conviction that God is leading them together, they will be unable to commit their lives to each other with the faith that God will make it possible for them to live up to that commitment.

These questions, in turn, lead the couple directly into chapter 3 and chapter 4, in which couples evaluate their relationship and work through a guide to make a solid decision about whether to marry.

5. *Sharing as a mentor:* For each of the four commitments, try to think of something you can share from your own marriage. For example, in the section on "receive your spouse" you could tell them about a time when you had to make a conscious decision after you were married to not regard your spouse as an enemy but as God's provision for your needs.

   In the section "leave your parents," you could talk about good and bad choices you've made in this area. This is one area where an unbiased adult can really help a young couple establish a healthy perspective. For example, you could talk to them about how to deal with the guilt a well-meaning parent may unfairly place upon them to come for visits or holidays.

   For "cleave to your spouse," you could tell about any temptations you've had to give up on your marriage, or about friends and family who got divorced because they were unable to meet their commitments.

6. The section on "become one flesh" brings up the topic of sex before marriage, and this is followed by a stronger section titled "A Special Word About Sexual Purity and Cohabitation." Ask the couple what they thought about this section. If the couple is having sexual relations, or if they are living together, this gives you another opportunity to challenge them to trust God and follow His plan. Also, ask if they completed the bonus project, "Purity Covenant," which is found after the Couple's Project. Challenge them to sign the covenant and pledge that they will not engage in sexual activity until they are married.

   If you are not satisfied with the couple's answers on this subject or with their commitment to purity, this is an appropriate time to ask if they are truly ready for marriage if they are unable to walk in obedience to God in such a critical area.

7. Suggested sequence for your meeting with the couple:

    a. Ask, "What were some things that you learned about God's purposes for marriage as you completed this chapter?"

    b. Ask, "What did you learn about yourself during this chapter?"

    c. Ask, "What did you learn about your fiancé(e) during this chapter?"

    d. For "Get the Picture," ask how they answered questions 1 and 2.

    e. For "Get the Truth," ask how they answered questions 4 through 12.

    f. Ask them how they would answer each of the two questions at the end of "Get the Truth":

        i. "Is Christ at the center of your life?" If their answer is no, you may need to explain the plan of salvation (see appendix on "Our Problems, God's Answers," or talk to them about how to build a more solid relationship with God).

       ii. "Is God calling you together as man and wife?" If they do not know how to answer this question, or if their answer seems vague, let them know that the next two chapters will provide the opportunity to explore this question.

Session 3

Evaluating Your Relationship

General Comments

1. This chapter is closely tied to chapter 4, "A Decision-Making Guide." Couples should complete both of these chapters individually and then discuss them together and with you. At the end of our notes for chapter 4, you will find a suggested sequence for your meeting with the couples to discuss both of these chapters.

2. Many premarried couples are so caught up in their emotions—either from the exhilaration of being in love or from the fear of commitment—that they are unable to think clearly about their relationship. This project is designed to help them do so by examining their compatibility on two different levels—spiritual and relational.

3. It is common for young married couples to realize that they differ significantly in their spiritual beliefs and commitment. One reason is that they never asked each other some difficult questions about spiritual compatibility. Many people will adopt a type of pseudo-spirituality in order to win over the person they love. For example, a young man may become interested in a woman and quickly notice that God is an important part of her life. He may not have a relationship with God, but he starts going to

church with her and shows interest in spiritual things. He learns how to sound spiritual, so he fools her into thinking he has a close relationship with Christ. After the wedding, however, he loses interest and leaves her feeling alone and betrayed.

Relational Compatibility

1. In the first part of this section we provide a very basic chart for evaluating how their personalities and temperaments mesh. This chart, however, is really included just for those couples who are completing the workbook on their own, apart from a pastor, counselor or mentor. There are much better tools available for you to use; two of the most popular are:

   ♥ Taylor-Johnson Temperament Analysis, Psychological Publications, Inc. (www.tjta.com)

   ♥ Prepare-Enrich couple assessment, Life Innovations (www.prepare-enrich.com)

   Both of these websites offer the opportunity to take the test online.

2. A primary goal here is to help couples understand their major similarities and differences and begin to discuss how these will affect their marriage. This is a good section to highlight how two people in marriage complete one another, as discussed in chapter 1.

Spiritual Compatibility

3. As the workbook states, there are two key questions couples need to answer:

♥ Are both of you Christians?
♥ Do you both share the same commitment to spiritual growth and to serving God?

The first question is critical because 2 Corinthians 6:14-15 warns against Christians entering into any partnership with unbelievers, because the relationship will be built on opposing values and goals. Building relationships on Christian values, trust and love is essential to the Christian life, especially in the most intimate of all human relationships—marriage. When a believer marries an unbeliever, the relationship begins with incompatibility in the most important area of life. Faith in God is the foundation for every aspect of a person's life—goals, expectations and values.

The second question addresses another important aspect of spiritual compatibility because there is a danger in one Christian marrying another who is much less mature and committed in the faith. This often leads to one of two things: Either the committed Christian will fall to the level of the other, or the committed Christian will develop growing frustration that the other is unwilling to grow stronger in faith.

4. If you completed the opening interview with the couple, you probably learned something of their spiritual background and were able to discern whether they were both Christians. If there is a problem in their spiritual compatibility and it was not confronted at that time, now is your opportunity as you meet with the couple and ask them how they answered questions 1 and 2.

5. If you realize that both people are not Christians, this is a great opportunity to explain the gospel. You can refer to appendix C, "Our Problems, God's Answers," which contains a clear presentation of how to know Christ.

We also urge you to exhort the couple to put the relationship on hold and concentrate first on establishing a relationship with God. If God eventually calls them together, their marriage will only be stronger if they've learned how to walk with Him.

6. If you find that one person is a believer but the other is not, exhort the couple to either end the relationship or put it on hold. They should certainly put off any wedding plans. The Christian may believe he or she may win the other to Christ, but this is a dangerous goal, because the nonbeliever may just put on a false front of repentance.

7. If both are Christians but there is a large gap in their spiritual maturity, encourage them to postpone marriage plans so they can take more time to see how God is working in the relationship. In some cases, they may need to stop seeing each other for a while.

Seeing Through the Fog

8. This section identifies seven factors that can easily hinder a couple in a serious relationship from seeing clearly: idealistic thinking, loneliness, sexual involvement, spiritual immaturity, wedding preparations, fear of failure, and fear of commitment.

Be aware that the fog may be so thick in premarried couples that they do not even recognize if any of these factors are causing problems. For example, if they are already well into preparing for the wedding, they may not realize that this can lead to problems if one of them has second thoughts about the marriage but doesn't want to back out because he or she fears how friends and family will react. This is your opportunity to talk to them about any factors that *you* have noticed!

Heeding Relational Red Flags

9. The final part of this section is a list of relational "red flags." These are serious problems that, if present in a relationship, will cause serious problems unless they are confronted and resolved before the wedding. In fact, some of these problems may lead you to strongly recommend ending the relationship.

    If one of these red flags is a concern for the couple you are mentoring, they probably will not want to discuss it together. We recommend talking to each person privately about this topic. Ask each if anything in this section applies to their relationship. Ask if there are any doubts about whether the relationship is healthy.

    Some couples are so caught up in their emotions and are moving so swiftly toward marriage that they fail to ask some tough questions or listen to their doubts about whether this relationship is really heading in the right direction. If you sense this is happening with the couple you are counseling, you will need to give them two strong challenges:

    First, *challenge the couple to seek guidance from God's Word and from trusted counselors.* Just as fog obscures reality by preventing us from spotting familiar buildings and landmarks, their emotions may prevent them from seeing the truth about their relationship.

    Read Psalm 119:105,130: "Your word is a lamp to my feet and a light to my path . . . the unfolding of Your words gives light; it gives understanding to the simple." Like an instruction book on how to operate your cell phone, the Scriptures are the Christian's instruction book for life. You cannot make a biblical decision apart from time spent in His Word.

    Proverbs 11:14 points to another source of guidance—trusted counselors: "Where there is no guidance the people fall, but in abundance of counselors there is victory."

What are their friends and family saying? If only one or two people don't like this match, you could attribute the objections to personality differences or selfishness. But if quite a few family and friends disapprove, it would be wise to learn why.

Second, *challenge the couple to take the time they need to make a good decision.* Ask if they think they've dated long enough to make a sound decision. Ask what they think would be the pros and cons of waiting another 6 to 12 months for the wedding.

They are, after all, about to commit themselves to loving and serving each other for a lifetime. It only makes sense to take the time they need to know whether they can truly make that commitment.

Session 4

A Decision-Making Guide

General Comments

1. This chapter continues the theme of evaluating a couple's relationship (chapter 3) and guides them in making the decision of whether they should marry. It helps them answer the question, "Is God leading us to be man and wife?"

    While we encourage them to complete this chapter shortly after completing chapter 3, couples should feel no pressure to make this decision yet. If you are counseling a couple who is struggling to determine God's direction, encourage them to read through this chapter and keep the concepts in mind as they complete the remainder of the workbook.

2. As with the previous chapter, we suggest the couples complete it on their own and then meet with you.

3. Many Christians have an incomplete understanding of how to discern God's will. Some seek God's direction on minute daily decisions, and look to discern God's supernatural leading in every circumstance of their lives. Others maintain that the Scriptures give us all we need to know about God's will for our lives, and it is up to us to use the sound mind God gives us to make the more difficult decisions.

This Decision-Making Guide is built upon two principles. First, we believe that the Bible contains God's direction for our daily lives. Second, He also has given us the Holy Spirit, who indwells us and leads and guides us. The Holy Spirit will speak to us through God's Word, through prayer, through godly counselors and through desires and circumstances to build within us a conviction of what God is leading us to do in certain situations.

4. At a later time, you might want to confirm this decision with each person individually. This is especially important if you sense that one person is not being totally honest or realistic in the decision.

5. Suggested sequence for discussing chapter 3 and chapter 4 with the couple:

   a. Begin by focusing on chapter 3 on "Evaluating Your Relationship." Ask, "What were some things you learned about your relationship by going through this chapter?"
   b. In the section on relational compatibility, ask how they answered questions 2 through 4 and 7.
   c. In the section on spiritual compatibility, ask how they answered question 8. Depending on how they answer, you can take this opportunity to challenge one or both of them to become a Christian or to walk more closely with Christ. Both subjects are covered in appendix C, "Our Problems, God's Answers."
   d. In the section on "Seeing Through the Fog," ask how they answered question 11.
   e. Moving on to chapter 4: Ask the couple if they understood the "Get the Truth" section, which explains the components of a biblical decision. Turn to the heading, "How Does Your Wheel Look?" Ask how they answered the questions there.

f. The Couple's Project guides couples through a decision-making process. Walk through the five steps of this process with them. Ask:

- ♥ Did each of you spend time alone with God? How much?
- ♥ Did you declare your willingness to follow God's will? Why do you think this is important?
- ♥ Have you honestly evaluated your relationship?
- ♥ Do you think you are God's provision for each other? Why?
- ♥ When do you think is the right time to marry, and why?

6. *Sharing as a mentor:* As you discuss chapters 3 and 4, take the opportunity to tell the couple about how you and your wife made the decision to get married. Talk about how you evaluated your relationship at the time and, if applicable, what you did to discern God's will. Be honest about what you did well and what mistakes you made as your relationship moved toward marriage.

Session 5

Authentic Communication

General Comments

1. Many couples experience such good communication during engagement that they cannot comprehend the possibility that they would have difficulty after they are married despite the fact they have probably observed communication problems in the lives of other married couples.

   This chapter is designed to give couples a few basics in communication and conflict resolution to help them avoid the "post-marriage letdown."

2. One major trend in our culture is an increasing difficulty in resolving conflict. Unresolved conflict leads to bitterness, isolation, physical and emotional abuse. At its worst, it leads to assault and death. In this chapter, couples will discuss their own history of resolving conflict and examine how they've worked out conflicts up to this point. They'll also learn about the importance of forgiveness.

3. In "Get the Picture," another story about Eric and Amanda alerts couples to how easily communication problems can develop early in a marriage.

4. "Get the Truth" presents three lessons about communication:

- ♥ Listening to understand
- ♥ Expressing to be understood
- ♥ Resolving conflict

Most of the material is pretty straightforward. For some couples it may not be new teaching; the question is how well they are applying it in their lives and in their relationship.

5. *Sharing as a mentor:* This is a great opportunity for you to take the biblical lessons of this chapter and bring them to life. Look through the three lessons about communication, and think back through your marriage to find examples of failures and successes in each area. Tell them about conversations in which you did not listen to your spouse, and when you did. Think of conflicts that you resolved well, and others that you did not. Tell about the consequences you've faced personally when you have not resolved conflict well.

   Also, tell them that many of the problems they will eventually face as a couple will come not from a lack of skill in listening or expressing or resolving conflict; it will come from *not communicating at all!* That's why this workbook has so much interaction built into it—to help couples do so much communicating before marriage that they will continue to do so after the wedding.

6. Suggested sequence for discussing this chapter with the couple:

   a. Ask, "What were some things you learned about communication and conflict as you completed this chapter?"
   b. Ask, "What did you learn about yourself during this chapter?"
   c. Ask, "What did you learn about each other during this chapter?"

d. Ask how they answered questions 1 and 2 after the Case Study in "Get the Picture."

e. Ask how they answered questions 2, 3 and 5 through 9 in "Get the Truth."

f. Ask how they answered questions 3 through 8 in the Couple's Project. Also, if someone has been previously married, discuss all the questions in "Special Questions for Those Who Were Previously Married."

Session 6

Roles and Responsibilities

General Comments

1. The purpose of this chapter is very simple—to provide couples with a biblical view of the roles of the husband and wife in marriage. This will be a difficult subject for many couples to discuss because for the last few decades our culture has relentlessly attacked biblical roles and sexual identity. Most adults in America today are very confused about the differences between men and women and about how the sexes should interact.

   As a mentor, it will be important for you to come to grips with what you believe the Bible says about roles for men and women in marriage. Two resources we highly recommend are *Rocking the Roles*, by Robert Lewis, and *Love and Respect,* by Emerson Eggerichs. These resources are available from FamilyLife by calling 1-800-FL-TODAY or by visiting our online store at www.familylife.com.

2. "Get the Picture" leads the couples through Scriptures that describe core roles for the husband (servant-leader) and wife (helper-homemaker). It's important to keep couples focused on what the Scriptures say and challenge them to avoid interpreting the Bible through contemporary eyes.

For example, when many people hear the word "leader" in the description of the core role for the husband, they often stereotype the leader in a marriage as a selfish tyrant who rules the house with an iron fist. The Bible, however, instructs husbands to love their wives "just as Christ also loved the church and gave Himself up for her" (Eph. 5:25). This is quite a different picture of leadership.

3. Many men have relinquished leadership of the home and have become passive. Indeed, this is the role many men who are marrying today will assume after they are married. A key challenge in this chapter is for men to accept responsibility and take the initiative in the home.

4. *Sharing as a mentor:* Tell them about the roles and responsibilities you have assumed in your marriage and how you have worked as a team. If you have not always lived according to biblical roles, describe what roles you once assumed and how you have changed. Be honest about mistakes you've made and struggles you've faced.

5. Suggested sequence for discussing this chapter with the couple:

   a. Ask, "What were some things you learned about roles as you completed this chapter?"
   b. Ask, "What did you learn about yourself during this chapter?"
   c. Ask, "What did you learn about your fiancé(e) during this chapter?"
   d. In "Get the Picture," ask how they answered question 2. If they had a difficult time answering the question, be prepared to prime the pump by mentioning some current movies or television shows that explore marriage relationships. Ask how husbands and wives are portrayed in a certain show or film.

e. Ask how they answered question 3 in "Get the Picture."

f. In the section "A Husband's Responsibilities" in "Get the Truth," ask, "What do you think it means for a husband to love his wife as Christ loves the church?" Then ask how they filled out the chart in question 5. Finally, ask if they understand what submission means in Scripture.

g. In the section "A Wife's Responsibilities" in "Get the Truth," ask, "What do you think it means for a wife to be a helper?" Then ask how they answered questions 10, 11 and 13.

6. In the Couple's Project, ask how they answered questions 2 and 3. Also, if someone has been previously married, discuss all the questions in "Special Questions for Those Who Were Previously Married."

7. Ask if the couple completed the bonus project in which they fill out a "Roles Position Statement." Encourage them to do so if they haven't. Explain that this will help them clarify what they understand about their roles, and they'll want to work on the project again after they are married.

Session 7

Money, Money, Money

General Comments

1. The goals of this chapter are to provide premarried couples with a basic scriptural foundation for handling money, and to guide them in discussing a few key issues that should be resolved before they are married.

   There are more than 2,000 verses in the Bible about finances, and for good reason: How we handle our money is a good indicator of who we are and what we believe. God uses this area to test our faith, to see whether we are willing to trust Him.

2. Many couples fail to discuss this area in much detail before marriage. In fact, talking about finances may make them feel uncomfortable. It should not come as a surprise, then, that a high percentage of couples who divorce within five years of their wedding state that conflict over finances was a major reason for their split.

   It is absolutely essential for couples to discuss their finances before marriage. If there is any problem in a relationship, chances are good that it will surface somehow in a financial decision. As the late financial counselor Larry Burkett said, "Money is the most common thing in our lives. If you're not communicating about money, you're not communicating about anything."

3. There are many reasons that couples face such intense conflict about finances after they are married:

   ♥ Many people grow up with good training in many areas of life, but they have not been taught how to handle their finances.

   ♥ A growing number of young people are falling into debt, especially consumer debt with credit cards. Premarriage counselors report they are seeing an increasing number of couples beginning marriage with a combined credit card debt of more than $10,000.

   ♥ God often brings opposites together in a marriage. A spender is often attracted to a saver, and vice versa. These differences quickly lead to conflict. (Special note: Contrary to the stereotype, husbands generally cause more problems than wives with overspending. Financial counselors report that, when women overspend, they do it on food and clothing. When husbands overspend, it's on big-ticket items such as cars and boats.)

   ♥ Many couples make unwise financial decisions in their first year of marriage. They purchase a new car or a home and take on large payments. Larry Burkett recommends that couples avoid purchasing a car or home during their first year of marriage.

   ♥ Couples often don't want to talk about finances, so they avoid discussing the very issues that could sabotage their relationship.

4. Because poor financial stewardship creates such a big problem in marriage, look closely for any signs of financial irresponsibility in those you counsel. One danger signal would be a large credit card debt. If you sense a big problem in

this area, recommend to the couple that they postpone their marriage for 6 to 12 months.

Chances are they will resist this idea, thinking they surely could quickly solve any problems in this area after they are married. This attitude, however, only proves your point—they don't realize how big a problem they will have after they are married.

5. In "Get the Picture" you will find the final installment in the Eric and Amanda saga. This Case Study presents, in detail, the different types of financial decisions they made after they were married.

6. In "Get the Truth," couples are guided through Scriptures that establish two critical truths they need to understand about their finances:

   ♥ God owns everything.
   ♥ We are stewards of money that God has entrusted to us.

From that base, couples discuss some specific, practical areas of financial management in which to apply those biblical principles.

7. *Sharing as a mentor:* Tell the couple about how you have handled finances during your marriage. Tell them how you organize your finances and how you make decisions as a couple.

   Be as honest as you can about what you've done well and what you've done poorly. Tell about some of your bad financial decisions—how and why you made them, and the consequences you faced.

   Also, challenge them about avoiding the materialism of our age. So many things we think we need are actually just desires influenced by advertising, by our emotions and by our own selfishness. In order to follow God and not the world, we need to take a hard look at our materialistic attitudes.

8. Suggested sequence for discussing this chapter with the couple:

    a. Ask, "What were some things you learned about finances as you completed this chapter?"
    b. Ask, "What did you learn about yourself during this chapter?"
    c. Ask, "What did you learn about your fiancé(e) during this chapter?"
    d. In "Get the Picture," ask how they answered question 3.
    e. In "Get the Truth," ask how they answered questions 2, 5, 7 and 9.

9. In the Couple's Project, ask how they answered questions 2 and 3. Also, if someone has been previously married, discuss all the questions in "Special Questions for Those Who Were Previously Married."

10. Ask if they completed the bonus section on setting a budget, and encourage them to do so if they have not.

Session 8

Intimacy:
Sexual Communication in Marriage

General Comments

1. The goal of this chapter is to give couples a biblical view about sex. They learn about God's purposes for sex, and they also learn about some differences between men and women in this area.

2. Many couples today almost have to be reprogrammed in this area. They have been so influenced by our culture that they are severely compromising God's standards about sexual purity. Hopefully, you've already discussed this issue with the couple by now. If you have not, now would be the time to do so.

3. This may be a difficult chapter for you as the mentor, because many of us are not accustomed to talking about sex to other people. Pray for wisdom about what to say, and for the ability to be transparent about this subject in an appropriate way.

4. We recommend that each couple obtain the book *Intended for Pleasure,* by Ed and Gail Wheat, and read it together during the last month before marriage.

5. "Get the Picture" seeks to help couples think through where they have learned about sex. Many of us learn from

the wrong sources and know little about what the Bible says. In fact, Christians are often stereotyped in the media as prudish, narrow zealots when it comes to this issue.

6. "Get the Truth" first presents the "right perspective" about sex: that it is God's idea, and that it is much more than a physical act—it's a process of intimate communication. Then it discusses God's purposes for sex—procreation, pleasure and protection. Finally, it presents a chart explaining differences between men and women in the sexual area.

7. *Sharing as a mentor:* Without becoming too explicit, tell them about some of the mistakes you have made as a couple. The section in "Get the Truth" about differences between men and women should provide you with some good ideas. Tell them about the expectations you had about sex going into marriage, and how those expectations influenced your attitudes and actions. Talk about things you have done to maintain romance and excitement in your marriage.

   At some point you should talk to each person individually. If you are mentoring as a couple, you and your spouse can talk with the person of the same sex. Ask more directly about what they anticipate in this area on the honeymoon and during the first year of marriage. Ask if they have any fears or any questions.

8. Suggested sequence for discussing this chapter with the couple:

   a. Ask, "What were some things you learned as you completed this chapter?"
   b. Ask, "What did you learn about yourself during this chapter?"
   c. Ask, "What did you learn about your fiancé(e) during this chapter?"

d. In "Get the Picture," ask how they answered questions 1 through 4.

e. In "Get the Truth," ask how they answered questions 5 through 9.

f. In the Couple's Project, ask how they answered questions 2 through 5. Also, if someone has been previously married, discuss all the questions in "Special Questions for Those Who Were Previously Married."

g. Be sure to mention the article at the end of the Couple's Project: "The Past: How Much Do I Share with My Fiancé(e)?" You don't need to read through it with them, but explain that if they have questions about how much they should share, they might want to come and consult with you first.

Premarital Couple Evaluation

Fill out this evaluation at the end of the course.

Premarital Couple: Mentoring Couple:

Male _____ Male _____

Female _____ Female _____

1. Circle the sessions that the premarital couple attended.

   1   2   3   4   5   6

   Any comments:

   _____
   _____
   _____
   _____
   _____
   _____
   _____
   _____

2. Circle the sessions in which the couple completed their homework.

   1   2   3   4   5   6

3. Did the couple receive sufficient input concerning the personality testing instrument that was used? ❑ Yes ❑ No

4. How many times did you meet with the couple outside the group?

   _____

   _____

5. Did the couple remain sexually pure during this time frame? ❑ Yes ❑ No

   Did you ask them a couple of times about this and get their specific responses? ❑ Yes ❑ No

6. Observations (check the box if the answer is yes):

	M	F
a. Do they communicate and listen well?	❑	❑
b. Are they flexible?	❑	❑
c. Are they teachable?	❑	❑
d. Do they have a realistic picture of a Christian marriage?	❑	❑
e. Do they have a reasonable understanding of each other's past?	❑	❑
f. Do they have good conflict-resolution skills?	❑	❑
g. Is Christ a vital part of their lifestyle?	❑	❑

   What other strengths does this couple exhibit?

   _____

   _____

   _____

   _____

   _____

   _____

   _____

   _____

Suggested areas of needed improvement:

_____

_____

_____

_____

_____

_____

_____

9. How do you think this couple grew in their relationship as they completed the workbook?

_____

_____

_____

_____

_____

_____

_____

10. Would you recommend that this couple marry? Why?

_____

_____

_____

_____

_____

Or, would you recommend they delay their marriage plans? Why? For how long?

_____

_____

_____

_____

_____

11. After marriage, what future recommendations would you specifically offer for this couple to further strengthen their relationship?

_____

_____

_____

_____

_____

_____

_____

About the Writers

David Boehi is a senior editor at FamilyLife. He is editor of the HomeBuilders Couples Series and writes and edits articles for FamilyLife's website, blogs, and e-newsletters. He and his wife, Merry, have two children and live in Little Rock, Arkansas.

Jeff Schulte is a fellow and director of the Sage Hill Institute, an initiative for authentic Christian leadership, and speaks nationally and internationally on biblical masculinity, fatherhood, spiritual formation, leadership and relational authenticity. He is a graduate of Yale University and earned two masters degrees from Western Seminary. He and his wife, Brenda, have six children.

Lloyd Shadrach is a teaching pastor at Fellowship Bible Church in Brentwood, Tennessee, which he co-planted in 1997. Previously he was a staff member with FamilyLife for 13 years. Lloyd is a graduate of Dallas Theological Seminary. He and his wife, Lisa, live in Franklin, Tennessee, with their three children.

Brent Nelson has served with a variety of ministries, including FamilyLife and Athletes in Action. He has earned degrees at Trinity College, Indiana University, and Trinity Evangelical Divinity School. He and his wife, Cassandra, live in Columbia, Tennessee, with their three children.

Dennis Rainey, general editor, is the president and cofounder of FamilyLife, a division of Campus Crusade for Christ. Dennis serves as the daily host of the radio program *FamilyLife Today*. He and his wife, Barbara, agree that their proudest achievement is their six children (with three more grafted in through marriage) and two grandchildren. The Raineys live in Little Rock, Arkansas.

If you'd like to build a stronger family, start by downloading a good blueprint.

We firmly believe that a stronger society starts with stronger marriages and families. That's why FamilyLife provides practical, biblical tools to help people become better husbands, wives and parents. With our help you can improve communication, bring back romance and give your family a good foundation to build on for years to come.

To get started, go to **FamilyLife.com**, where you can find all of our resources and download a free subscription to our enewsletter, *The Family Room*.

FAMILY LIFE®
Help for today. Hope for tomorrow.

Know Where You're Headed Before You Walk Down the Aisle

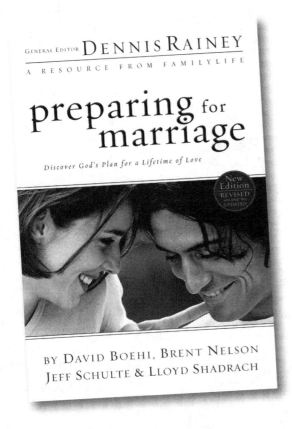

Preparing for Marriage
Dennis Rainey, General Editor
ISBN 978.08307.46408
ISBN 08307.46404

You're in love, and it's the real thing. Now, as you plan your wedding celebration, it is time to lay the foundation for a lifetime of love and romance. Today you can begin the important, lifelong task of building a strong Christian marriage. Created by FamilyLife, one of America's leading marriage and family ministries, *Preparing for Marriage* is a dynamic, comprehensive program designed to help you prepare for life together after the cake is cut and the guests head home. Learn about God's unique blueprints for marriage. In eight sessions, you will learn how to discern God's will for your relationship; handle your finances and plan for the future; clarify your roles and responsibilities; establish a positive, loving sexual relationship; deal with issues, expectations and family histories; and evaluate as a couple your readiness for marriage. Don't just plan your wedding . . . prepare for your marriage!